OVERCOMING THE TRAP OF INSECURITY

My Journey Towards a Fearless and Fulfilling Life

Jo-Ann May

THE TRAP OF INSECURITY. Copyright © 2023. Jo-Ann May. All Rights Reserved.

Printed in the United States of America.

No portion of this book may be reproduced, stored in a retrieval system, or transmitted in any form or by any means, except for brief quotations in printed reviews, without the prior written permission of DayeLight Publishers or Jo-Ann May.

DAYELight
PUBLISHERS

ISBN: 978-1-958443-41-5

Edited by: Stacey Samuels

To the Most High God, the One who knew me before I was formed and prepared good works for me to do in advance. May You be pleased with this offering.

Table of Contents

Preface 7
Acknowledgement 9
INTRODUCTION 13
Chapter 1: The Day Everything Changed 17
Chapter 2: Insecure For Sure 25
Chapter 3: Lonely Is The Night 31
Chapter 4: Fearful 37
Chapter 5: Identity Crisis 41
Chapter 6: Loveless 47
Chapter 7: Let It Go 55
Chapter 8: A New Day Has Dawned 59

Preface

There are many stories on the shelves of libraries or in the digital space that deal with the human condition in all its various forms. This book is meant to explore the topic of insecurity, its effect on my life, how I handle it, and to offer potential solutions for those who may be struggling with the same thing. This is not a self help book or a prescriptive text. This was written as an act of obedience to the Lord and I pray that it blesses each person who reads through its pages.

While expounding on the things I went through, it mentions some people in my life and the effect that they had on me. It is not meant to cast them in a negative light, it does however, explore some of the feelings I had and the wounds I experienced from varying interactions over the course of my life. I can honestly say that those referenced: mainly my immediate family and former spouse, held no ill will toward me. The fact of life is that somewhere along the journey, we experience hurt and pain. Most of the time, it is not the intention of the other person to do us damage. As we go through life, we come up against or face situations that leave us feeling that the outcome was less than desirable. When our expectations are not met, it causes pain and if we are not careful, it reorients our thinking.

I encourage you to take your time and make your way through it slowly. It is my sincere hope that through my vulnerability you will feel seen and know that you are not alone. You don't have to walk through this on your own, help is available. I pray that my God, would meet you right where you are, bring comfort to your soul and guide you in the way you should go.

Acknowledgement

The process of writing a book includes so much more than I originally thought and I wouldn't have made it to the end without the help and encouragement of a few people that I'd like to highlight.

To Rashida, the very first person I shared this God idea with, even before I was convinced it was really God, thank you. You helped me get past the initial fear and start typing. Your belief in my ability to actually do this was the push I needed and your feedback on the first few chapters was fundamental to helping establish a good base to build on.

Pastor Marsha Davidson, my mentor and dear sister in the Lord, I am grateful to you for helping me discern more clearly the voice of the Lord. You have taught me principles that played a vital part in the healing journey. Thank you for your consistent prayers.

To the one who selflessly gave of her time to edit what I thought was the complete first draft, Kenia, you rock! You helped keep me accountable to finish this book and sent encouraging messages reminding me that I had something to say. Your insights have helped reframe the way I approached this project and your willingness to lend me your device for weeks while I went through your recommendations can never be forgotten. You are a true friend indeed.

To the bestie I never knew I had until I needed him the most, thank you for believing in me every step of the way. You never doubted and constantly reminded me that I could do it even when I felt like giving up. Your constancy has been a gift I never knew I needed. Thank you Craig for being you.

Mom and dad, your openness and willingness to have the hard conversations and discuss the way I experienced things growing up has truly been a blessing. It has made this process much easier and less angsty. I honour you both for being the amazing parents you are and for giving me the most important thing I could have in life, a good example of what it means to be a christian.

To my favourite brother in the whole wide world, Aaron, thank you for being there for me always. Though our relationship hasn't always been rainbows and butterflies, I'm grateful to have you as my brother and I'm thankful that we've come such a long way from those rough teenage and early adult years. You are a shining example of dedication and diligence. May you continue to bring joy to those around you and excel in all your endeavours.

Stacey, my final editor and sister. How can words ever fully express the support you've been to me in this time? You have provided guidance practically and spiritually and really helped me bring this project together. Your dedication and excellence have not gone unnoticed and I thank you deeply for all the work you have put in. I have no idea how I would have been able to pull this off without you.

INTRODUCTION

For I know the thoughts that I think toward you, saith the Lord, thoughts of peace, and not of evil, to give you an expected end.

Jeremiah 29:11

It's 11:17 p.m. on January 5th 2022 and here I sit, trying to figure out how to tell this story. A story of a woman who, for most of her life, allowed insecurity to rob her of so many great things. Meet Josie, a beautiful, intelligent, talented, vibrant, woman in her late thirties who is on the brink of getting a divorce after just over six years of marriage. What went wrong? How did things turn out this way? Looking back at the last few years, she wonders, "what have I done to deserve this?"

The truth is that this didn't happen overnight. As a matter of fact, this started years before she even met her soon to be ex-husband. Little did she know that the unresolved and oft undetected issues from her past would cloud her judgment and affect her ability to make healthy choices in life.

Introduction

As a little girl, Josie was known for being joyful and energetic, which quickly earned her the nickname Joey the kangaroo as she was always bouncing around from one thing to the other. She was full of love and laughter and enjoyed getting into harmless mischief with any other willing children who were around.

One day, unknown to Josie, that carefree love for life and all its wonders would begin to slip away. To say she could identify when it all happened would be a lie. All she knew was that one day, she woke up an adult wondering when life had taken this turn and if or how she would ever get back to those days when she was happy.

Josie, the adult, is yours truly. Follow me on a journey through my life as I navigate the murky waters of insecurity in the hopes of finding joy, peace, and fulfillment in purpose. This is not intended to be prescriptive nor is it an exposition on all the different ways that insecurities are formed or developed. Instead, this is an honest reflection of my life, what I went through, and where I am now. All is not perfect today, but I am a far cry from where I used to be and I continue to put in the work to make necessary changes to improve the quality of my life and relationships.

It is my hope that through this book, many would come to recognize the widespread negative impact of insecurity on lives and be a resource for those who desire to start on the road to moving beyond the lies that have held them back for so long. I pray this gives young girls and women in general, hope; hope for a better tomorrow. We cannot undo what has already gone but we have the power to determine how we move forward.

Chapter 1

The Day Everything Changed

And we know that all things work together for good to them that love God, to them who are the called according to his purpose.

Romans 8:28

Have you ever woken up and wondered out loud; "What the heck?!? How did I end up here???" If you have, welcome to the club.

I used to think those things only happened in movies, and I remained blissfully unaware of how I was really feeling until the day I quite literally woke up wondering how I ended up in a situation where I was so unhappy that, unknown to many around me, I began thinking of ways I could escape. It all sounds dramatic, but there had to be more to life than just existing, going through life in a fog with no sense of direction or purpose and feeling like I was a burden to those around me. This couldn't be all there was.

> It wasn't always like this.

Surely, I had missed my exit somewhere along the highway of life and I was now hopelessly lost with no GPS signal and that stupid automated voice screaming at me that it was rerouting and I needed to take the next exit. Except there was no exit. No matter how much further I drove, there was no exit in sight, no off roads on either side, just one, straight, narrow and very dark road.

It wasn't always like this. A few hundred miles back I had taken a turn that I was certain was the right one. I had a way of determining, against all direction and a few road signs saying otherwise, that I knew the way. Radio blaring, gears shifting, wind in my hair while speeding into the great unknown of what I was convinced was my happily ever after.

Six plus years later, I've run out of gas, there's smoke coming from under the hood of my car and there's an infernal knocking under my feet that I just can't seem to figure out. What's worse? There's nothing and no one in sight. I've almost single handedly become stranded on the side of the road while my car wheezes and putters along hoping that

I'll be able to salvage something from the situation. I've come to a stop and decided to retrace the steps in my mind to see where I went wrong. When did I zig instead of zag?

I remember being happy once, deliriously so, without a care in the world but somewhere along the way, that changed. What happened? Was there one pivotal thing that caused everything to go belly up? No, I think not. What I have found are a myriad of smaller moments that ushered me here. A detour here, a missed turn there. They all began to add up to determine how I came to be so far off track. Somehow, I convinced myself along the way that this was what life was supposed to look like: the career, the husband, the house, the involvement in church. To those looking on, I'm sure they thought I had it all. As far as anyone knew, the only thing missing was the baby. I've heard it all, *"What are you guys waiting on? Please don't let those good genes go to waste! Your expiration date is coming, you need to do something quickly."* We'd been trying since we got married but it just hadn't happened.

Somewhere between playing Mother Goose in my kindergarten graduation play and auditioning for a solo part in the sixth-grade graduation song, something in me broke. I'm not sure what it was or how it came to be that way definitively. I only know that looking back, those five to six years signaled a big change in me and my approach to life. Gone was Joey the kangaroo and in came the era of JoJo. My joy was gone, that sense of wonder with which I viewed the world, the belief that I could do anything and be anyone I wanted to be. During the course of those years, my self-esteem and sense of self-worth became so imperceptibly eroded that I woke up more than twenty years later and realized that something was missing. I lost myself along the way and I was struggling to remember who I was, while yearning for those days to return.

I wanted to be that little girl who found joy in the smallest things, whose eyes lit up with wonder and amazement at the beauty of nature. I longed to get that back but, I knew that after so long, it wouldn't be easy. I would have to dive deep into the past and spend some time stitching tattered pieces of memories together to find where the treasure was hidden, where the shipwrecked parts of my life had been scattered.

> I lost myself along the way...

I grew up in a home with both parents and one brother who was three years my senior. My earliest recollection of life was happy, extremely over the top happy. There were trips to the country to visit family friends and new places to explore. I enjoyed music and drama and everything school related. I was friendly and outgoing, always ready to be involved in some activity or other. It came as no surprise then, that when it was time to graduate from kindergarten, that I would be cast in the play about Mother Goose. I can't remember which character I played, but I do remember searching through mommy's closet to find the perfect costume. It was a long white skirt with yellow, blue, pink, and black shapes all over. That was the last time I remember feeling totally free to be me in all my glory; young, exuberant, and full of life!

The next few years were a blur and soon enough after graduation, the family moved from our first home into a family house with aunts and uncles, and dad went off to further his education. The summer before he left the four of us took a trip to England, where we had an amazing time. I remember visiting the zoo, making new friends and crossing the English Channel on a ferry to take a one-day trip through France, Belgium, and Holland. Of course, there were some unpleasant moments but overall, we had a blast and I believe this is when my love for travel was born. Upon our return home to

Jamaica, dad went off to school and my brother, mom, and I settled in our 'new' home and got into a routine. We saw dad most weekends as he would either come home or we would go to visit him. My brother and I would occasionally get to spend the weekend with him at his school, but it just wasn't the same as having him home with us. I longed for our family to go back to the way it was with daddy being present everyday and readily accessible at home.

Unawares, a void began to grow in me. My brain understood, as much as it could at the time, that this was something he had to do and something that would give us a better life at the end of the day. But my heart didn't. I began to feel as though he liked the people he went to school with more than us and that he preferred spending time with them. I wondered why he couldn't just go and come home every day like others did. Why did he have to board? Was he trying to get away from me? Was there something I did that made him want to escape? I just didn't get it; and so with each week or month that passed, though we saw him frequently, I began to feel a little less important to him, a little less valuable. Did he

> Was he trying to get away from me?

deliberately move away just to hurt me? Of course not, but that didn't change the way I felt.

It's interesting that I never realized that was how I felt at the time. Before writing this book, all these unresolved feelings were never acknowledged, much less articulated. Unearthing these issues have come little by little, over time and I can only say that the Lord, in His grace, has seen it fit now to bring them to light.

Chapter 2

Insecure For Sure

The Lord thy God in the midst of thee is mighty; he will save, he will rejoice over thee with joy; he will rest in his love, he will joy over thee with singing.

Zephaniah 3:17

For those who know me or have interacted with me in various capacities, it may come as a shock that I struggle with insecurity. For years I donned a mask, presenting as confident and assertive in many circles with only those closest to me knowing that something was amiss every now and then. The depth and full scope of my battle remained hidden from everyone for a very long time. I hardly even realized it myself, so how could I tell anyone?

What I did know, was that there seemed to be a disparity between thought and reality; a misalignment of sorts. There had been days when I looked at myself in the mirror and said, 'You, girl, are beautiful! There's no way you should be this hot!' and others, many others, when I felt like I was just your average cup of Jo, nothing special, trying to make my way through life like the rest of the world. While I'll admit that this isn't a battle I've fully conquered yet, I'm a far way from where I used to be.

I believe that the tiny, unintended seeds of feelings of not being loved or valued and a deep fear that I was no longer wanted, were planted at that early stage in my life and since then, I've been sporting a full blown insecurity tree. Little by little, with different interactions that were either negative or perceived to be so, things happened that acted as fertilizer, providing mulch and water, which sent the roots deeper and the branches ever closer to the sun. The tree was thriving. It's funny how the little things that happen in our lives shape us, so much so that we can't remember how we were or who we used to be before. And although they have such a profound effect, most people are unable to pinpoint or even remember in detail the majority of these happenings.

> You girl, are beautiful!

You see, the thing about insecurity is that it starts off so covertly that most times trying to pinpoint its genesis is near impossible. Slowly but surely, it erodes self-confidence and the healthy measure of self-esteem a person should have to maintain and preserve their value to themselves and others around them. This can easily result in the development of an unhealthy desire to please people and lead you into a cycle of making poor choices in every area of your life. For me, it was most evident in my relational life, especially in encounters with the opposite sex.

Having been raised in a Christian home, I was taught the virtue of preserving my virginity until I was married and there was a time, when I held fast to that teaching. I remember thinking about how beautiful it would be to give my husband that gift. Unfortunately, when I gave that gift away at the age of nineteen, the effects of insecurity and low self-esteem were already in play and had been for quite some time. The act was just a physical manifestation of what had already happened in my mind and was the beginning of a series of many sexual encounters that would see me giving myself away time and time again in search of love and affirmation, only to end up worse off than when I started. I was stuck. Caught in an unforgiving cycle of exchanging my body for a momentary high that wasn't usually achieved. Many of these interactions took place after drinking heavily and while I was often on the receiving end of the advances of men, I initiated my fair share of one night encounters. Although I was under the influence of alcohol on many occasions, I was always aware of what was happening and went along with it.

> Insecurity makes you feel as though you have no choice.

Insecurity makes you feel as though you have no choice. It whispers, that you were the one who brought this on yourself and that it would be unfair and unreasonable to say no. It grabs you, holds you hostage and requires a ransom. Interaction after interaction, it demands you pay with pieces of your self-worth. After a while, you see yourself as having no value and you 'know' that nobody else values you. You find yourself willing to do just about anything to feel like somebody cares.

To those looking on, you seem to have it all together, to be in full control. I became accustomed to wearing a mask. I learned how to appear confident, how to speak as if I was in total control, and knew exactly what I wanted. I had all the right words, mannerisms, and the perfect style to suit my brand. I knew exactly what I wanted to portray and did so seemingly effortlessly. I used my body subtly to get attention, never quite going overboard but dallying right on the edge of appearing to not care what anybody else thought, while being sexy as hell. It was a fine line to walk but I navigated it like a pro.

Over the years I have come to learn a lot about insecurity. Firstly, it is no respecter of persons. Insecurity doesn't care if you are rich or poor, tall or short, black, white, or any shade in between. It uses similarities and differences equally to cause you to feel as though you are 'less than'. It is not logical or rational, and does not care whether the words said to you at any given point in time were meant with the best intentions or not.

Insecurity taints everything. Every interaction, every relationship, every word to feed the lie used to keep you bound. It is an invisible prison whose bars are no less real than the ones found in a state penitentiary. It is solitary confinement. A place where you are left alone with only those thoughts to keep you company. A space cut off from interaction with the outside world, where nothing and no one can reach you.

Insecure For Sure

What most people don't realize is that while insecurity seems to cause a person to shy away from others, appearing to want to disappear and for there to be no focus on them; it reinforces that very thing and turns a bright light on the individual in question. It thrives in excessive introspection and grows due to an inordinate amount of self focus. Insecurity, my friends, is really an issue of pride. It causes you to spend so much time thinking about yourself and what you believe others think of you, that all the compliments and kind words of others are viewed through a dirty glass. There must always be an ulterior motive, something that somebody wants from you in exchange for their platitudes. Nothing good is real and lasting.

Chapter 3

Lonely Is The Night

Turn thee unto me, and have mercy upon me; for I am desolate and afflicted.

Psalms 25:16

Living with insecurity can feel a bit like having a roommate that doesn't communicate well. They never let you know when they are going out or will be late getting in. In the same way, you never quite know when it will show up and mess up your best laid plans.

Imagine waking up one bright and sunny morning, clear blue skies as far as the eye can see. You get out of bed, take a shower, get ready for the day ahead, look in the mirror and think to yourself 'Ah yes, today is going to be a great day.'. You like what you see and how you feel. You step out the door and head towards the car. You notice your neighbour outside and normally they would say hi but this morning they don't. You decide not to let that ruin your day so instead of wondering why they haven't said hi, you go ahead and say good morning, only there's no response. You know you said it loud enough to be heard so why didn't they say anything? You begin to wonder if there's something you did to cause them to be non responsive toward you, but nothing comes to mind. Maybe, you think to yourself, maybe they're just having a bad day. You try to put it out of your mind and move on with your day, but as the day progresses you realize that you're feeling a little low and you can't seem to figure out where it all went wrong. It makes no logical sense that an interaction you put out of your mind has derailed your entire day. It really wasn't a big deal so why does it have so much power over you, you wonder.

This is the trap of insecurity. Taking something that is going on with someone else and making it about you; how you feel, what role you played, what you could have done differently. This is the hook. You bite the bait when you begin to consider the circumstances and without realizing, you find yourself entering deep introspection trying to figure out what your role in it was. This is a lonely place to be. Don't get me wrong, introspection has its place. But when you begin to think that you hold enough power to so drastically affect other people's decisions and by extension life, the stench of pride begins to rise.

Insecurity isolates you. It makes you think that no one will ever be able to understand what you're going through or how you are feeling. There are many different responses to this feeling of isolation. I chose to respond by adjusting my behaviours in order to better fit in with a particular crowd. I became a master of observation, watching to see which group of persons best fit in each situation. I assessed others, found similarities, and played to my strengths in those groupings while downplaying the parts of me I felt didn't quite suit them. In other settings I displayed other parts of me and was able to get along well with those persons too. To me, it never felt like manipulation. After all, I truly liked hanging around different sets of people and felt that I was someone who could be all things to all people. What it was, in reality, was self-rejection. I determined that all of me wasn't good enough to be seen by all persons, so I only showed the 'relevant' parts to each set or group. This was great for ensuring I had a wide cross-

> I was someone who could be all things to all people. What it was, in reality, was self-rejection.

section of people to talk and interact with, but it also meant that I had very few or in some settings, no real friends. No one knew the real me.

I became so accustomed to hiding elements of me that over time I forgot who I was. I was fluid, a chameleon, changing my colours to suit my surroundings. I never felt that people really liked me and in part I blamed them. It felt as though people were being fake. I couldn't figure out why people liked me and whether they wanted to truly be around me or they were just around me for what they thought they could get. I had no idea why I even thought that, because as far as I was concerned, I had nothing to give. I wasn't rich, I didn't have an active social life, I wasn't particularly cool. I was average or just above average in school and I looked alright I supposed, but there really wasn't anything special about me in my eyes. Insecurity made sure I kept myself from forming lasting bonds with others by always feeling as though I wasn't good enough and had nothing to offer.

> I never felt that people really liked me and in part I blamed them.

There was, I thought, one upside. Guys liked me. That worked for me since I didn't think girls really wanted to be my friends and I always had tomboyish tendencies. This meant that I always had more male friends than female friends. We got on better and generally had more fun without all the complications of comparisons, which were always present around females. I felt I could just be me around the guys, no putting on shows, no trying to fit in, just being. To them, I was the cool girl they could talk to about anything, who looked good and was down-to-earth. This was a win-win as far as I was concerned. I didn't have to worry about the snide remarks, the rolled eyes and the pretense. No dressing up and trying to keep up with the latest fashion or feeling out of place with the "in crowd" of girls. I was neatly placed and happy in my world of male friends.

Chapter 4

Fearful

For God hath not given us the spirit of fear; but of power, and of love, and of a sound mind.

2 Timothy 1:7

What almost everyone around me didn't know is that I lived in fear of being unmasked; of being called out as a fraud. Fear had me firmly in its grasp and was loath to let me go. Even in writing this book, fear has been a major player; something I have had to push to overcome. Wondering if what I am going through is enough to write a whole book about. If anybody is going to be interested in what I have to say, whether or not it will be engaging so people will want to read it. Do I even have enough wisdom to offer for it to be helpful to those who read it? Because who wants to read a book that offers no solutions?

Those questions highlight my fear of failure, but make no mistake, the fear of success is just as actively at work. Suppose people really do like it and I am invited to talk about it in different arenas, will I be able to do that? I like being in the background, will this thrust me into the spotlight? What if I'm invited to speak and people realize that I'm not a great speaker? At every turn, there is fear.

Similarly, growing up, fear played a major role in most if not all my decisions; mainly the fear of people and what they would think of me. Whenever those closest to me questioned my choices or decisions I made, it would hurt but I rarely let on. Their disapproval slowly ate away at my confidence and caused me to question myself. I struggled with knowing when to assert myself and when to acquiesce for a peaceful life. This battle shut down some of the very things that made me, me.

> At every turn there is fear.

I learned to become a people pleaser. Carefully noting what was acceptable in different social settings, I aligned myself with situations and people that I thought would require less work, or where I thought the consequences of being found out would be less severe. I found comfort and ease in interacting with those who were less formally learned than myself, making for what I thought was a fair exchange. A glimpse into their lives, an opportunity to learn and experience what they went through and to offer assistance, a helping hand wherever I could.

I purposely stayed away from those who were more learned, more affluent, and more connected because I felt that it would be easier for them to see that I didn't fit in with them. I relegated myself to being a friend of so and so, an attachment or appendage, instead of asserting myself as an individual and always felt awkward interacting with those third party friends. Even in situations where I was invited by the relevant persons, I felt uncomfortable, constantly thinking that they were just trying not to make me feel bad and extended a pity invitation to me. I never viewed myself as good enough to be consistently around people of influence, movers and shakers in society.

My fear caused me to self isolate and grow resentful as I noticed that others used these relationships or 'links' to get ahead in life. I wondered why I wasn't fortunate enough to get things because of who I knew. The truth was that oftentimes I was not bold enough to ask. I hid from them, cowering in fear, wondering if they would think I was only using them to get ahead. Insecurity skewed my thought processes to the point where I felt that asking anything of anyone would be interpreted as me taking advantage of the relationship. It never occurred to me that reciprocity is a healthy part of relationships. In fact, it became the norm for me to be excessively accommodating of others out of fear that I would not be accepted otherwise.

> ...reciprocity is a healthy part of relationships.

Chapter 5

Identity Crisis

But now thus saith the LORD that created thee, O Jacob, and he that formed thee, O Israel, Fear not: for I have redeemed thee, I have called thee by thy name; thou art mine.

Isaiah 43:1

Insecurity doesn't walk alone, along the way it picks up pals like fear, loneliness, and identity crisis. I hid different parts of myself to match the setting I was in. Who I *really* was remained a mystery even to me. I had become so used to adapting to different personalities and situations that I had no idea who I would be existing in a space by myself. What were *my* likes, dislikes, passions, and desires?

From an early age I was compared with others at school in the hope that it would be a motivational tool, pushing me to excel, to be better.

Unfortunately, the tactic did not work but served instead to erode my sense of self worth as I began thinking that I was not as good as others, that there was something wrong with me.

Being a tomboy in those days was highly frowned upon and a tomboy is certainly what I was. This did not bode well for me especially as it related to the older women in my life. I frequently refused to wear dresses, skirts, pink, and most traditionally female garb and would often do the exact opposite of what a young lady was supposed to do, much to the chagrin of my dear mother. I ran around climbing trees, sitting on walls, getting dirty and doing pretty much everything the boys did. My preference was hanging out with the boys because I wasn't particularly a fan of frills and lace and the things the boys were doing were just so much more fun. This is not to say that I didn't have girls that I played with but somehow I ended up around the boys more.

> I just did not fit the profile, the mold.

Over the years, this caused my mother much distress. My mom was a woman raised to be proper. A former dancer with perfect posture and a graceful gait, the epitome of a lady. Yet, here I was, obviously her daughter as the resemblance was strong but so seemingly wayward. I just did not fit the profile, the mold. That's not to say that I was a terror however, time after time I sensed my mother's frustration and she constantly pleaded for me to not be so contrary. While she did her best to raise a proper young lady with impeccable manners and posture, I just would not conform.

Deep within, the sustained complaints about my 'wayward' behaviour caused me to think that I was not enough, that there was something fundamentally wrong with the way I was. Why couldn't I just be like the others, the ones that were prim and proper? I couldn't reconcile being fearfully and wonderfully made with the way I felt when being compared to others or being reprimanded for my unladylike manner. Often times when remarks were passed about the way I was, my rapid fire response would be, 'Factory Fault', implying that truly I thought that maybe God made a mistake with me.

The only thing I knew, for sure, was that there were fears. Those were clear as day and ranged from fear of failure to fear of success, and just about everything in between. I remember being known as my brother's sister, my father's daughter et al. I was always somebody else's someone. A sister, daughter, girlfriend, friend, classmate, worshiper, leader, mechanic, wife, and the list goes on. One label stuck on top of another and another and I wore each one with pride.

Soon I began to notice that I resented the idea of being known as an extension of someone else. Wasn't I a person too? Didn't I have value? Didn't I bring anything to the table of each interaction? I struggled with wondering if I was only good for one off encounters with people and I realized that when I ran into these same people in other settings, I would shrink back and hide so I wouldn't be seen. I didn't want them to feel as though they had to acknowledge me and I didn't want to experience the awkwardness of saying hi only to be looked at with no recognition. In a way, I became proactively aloof pretending not to see people I knew so I wouldn't feel the shame of not being remembered.

> I rarely took an opportunity to show people who I was or what I had to offer.

My desire to be an individual, a standalone person, was great and looking back now, I can say, has robbed me of potentially rich friendships. I would get so caught up in not wanting to be known as this or that person's anything that I never asserted myself. I rarely took an opportunity to show people who I was or what I had to offer. But truly, how could I when I didn't even have a handle on who I was or what I brought to the table? Only recently have I begun to see that most of that was in my head. I was so concerned with what *I* thought people were thinking about me that I never really stopped to find out from them what they actually thought.

Chapter 6

Loveless

The LORD hath appeared of old unto me, saying, Yea, I have loved thee with an everlasting love: therefore with lovingkindness have I drawn thee.

Jeremiah 31:3

It was while on this journey of discovery that I came to realize, I didn't really know what love was. I had experienced a form of love but not love in its truest form or sense. That is not to say that I wasn't loved by family or friends, but more of a realization that though the words were frequently spoken, I had no real understanding of it. I came face to face with my deep sense of lack. I found a hole that I didn't know was there; a chasm into which all the reassurances of love and worth seemed to disappear.

I came to see that no matter how often I was told I was loved, somehow I just never truly believed it to be so. I frequently felt like a disappointment to those close to me. I felt like a drain on their resources and erroneously believed that they only loved me if and when I was able to provide some kind or type of reciprocal value. In essence, my experience of love was transactional. I was loved and celebrated as long as I met the expectations of those around me. When I didn't quite measure up, there were looks of disapproval, reprimands and encouragement to come back in line.

Interestingly enough, my love for others had not been that way. I often extended myself far beyond what was reasonable to ensure those I cared for felt loved; many times denying my own desires for their benefit. I thought that if I could meet their needs, maybe I would be worthy of their love. If I gave all I could to the relationship, even if they initially didn't feel the same way, they would eventually come around. They would come to see that I brought value to their lives and want to keep me in it.

> I often extended myself far beyond what was reasonable...

Having lost myself, a self I wasn't sure of, became commonplace. It was par for the course. I adapted to my surroundings, becoming whatever was needed in that space until either the relationship died a natural death or I couldn't bear it any more and pulled away leaving yet another piece of myself behind. I often felt like I was the one who gave so much to the relationship, the one always trying to make it work. I began to realize that when I stopped making the effort, the other person never usually reached out. In fact, more often than not, I wouldn't hear from them again. Each occurrence only served to cement the belief in my mind that I was not valuable.

I yearned to be loved, to be desired, to be accepted for who I was, flaws and all. To experience a love that surpassed my mistakes and covered my missteps. I tried to identify when the transactional nature of the love I knew came to be; to unearth the roots of the tree that had damaged the very foundation of my life. This has been a painful journey thus far. One that has shone light on the deepest, darkest recesses of my mind and exposed things I never knew were there.

You see, our experiences in life, from the time we are born, shape our understanding of the world and the different concepts, ideologies, and philosophies we come to call our own. Each interaction produces in us either a building block reinforcing what we already believe, or a sledgehammer that breaks it down. From the moment of birth, our encounters with those in our sphere of existence begin to teach us, laying the foundation for what we believe love is, what we come to see as acceptable and unacceptable behaviour, and whether or not we matter or have value to those around us. This is true of all humans.

> ...each person is responsible for how they handle the information presented to them..

Over time and with the introduction of new concepts in the thought world, we have the opportunity to evolve by applying these principles based on research or deeper levels of understanding that comes a a result of revelation or trial and error. However, each person is responsible for how they handle the information presented to them in its various formats. With the rapid increase in the use of social media, more information is available to us than ever before in bite sized, easily digestible pieces. Of course, our desire and ability to digest same is based on a few factors.

The primary things we learned and the way those around interacted with each other and with us, molded our understanding of the world and dictated the way we expected to be dealt with. This revelation came to me during the course of my marriage. I began to see that while my husband and I seemed to be on completely different pages, it wasn't a deliberate attempt on either part to frustrate the other. It was that we could only give as much as we had to give and what we had to give was a direct result of how we navigated life up to that point. The truth is that he loved me the only way he knew how.

> ...as I deliberately told myself that I was precious to my mother, something began to change in me.

I also came to realize that there were lies I'd grown to believe. That with the passage of time, things that started out as a joke had become an entire belief system. It was a testament to Proverbs 18:21 'Death and life are in the power of the tongue: and they that love it shall eat the fruit thereof.' These lies were not just things others spoke to or about me but things I had rehearsed to myself; repeating time and time again and usually with a laugh.

There was a running joke that my brother, was my mother's favourite, that he was 'precious'. I was the one who gave him the nickname from a book and subsequent movie trilogy from 2001. For over twenty years I had been eating away at my own already damaged value and self-worth by implying that since he was 'precious', I was not. Initially I thought it was silly. Surely I knew that it wasn't true, my mother loved me just as much as she loved my brother. I was convinced that this couldn't really be a problem but as I deliberately told myself that I was precious to my mother, something began to change in me.

Another light bulb that switched on for me in the process, was the awareness that brokenness attracts brokenness. What this meant for me was that the areas in my life that were broken, the lies that I had believed about not being worthy of love actually attracted persons with similar beliefs and areas of brokenness. In the same way, the wounds that were unintentionally inflicted, drew people to me who would continue to do damage of the same nature, ensuring that I never got out of that destructive cycle. This is not to say that it was deliberate and sinister on their part, I believe that they were mostly innocent and had good motives but because of our respective brokenness, we were susceptible to the devices of the enemy.

As those roots were unearthed, I began to see things from a different perspective. Healing began to take place in my heart and broken areas started to come together. I can't tell you the freedom that I began to experience once these realizations came to the fore. No, everything wasn't magically okay but I had a point from which to start. It was as if the dark clouds began to roll back and beams of light came streaming through, illuminating my world.

Chapter 7

Let It Go

Then said Jesus, Father, forgive them; for they know not what they do.

Luke 23:34a

I always prided myself on being one who was ready and willing to apologize and subsequently forgive whenever I had committed an infraction or felt that there was an injustice meted out to me. I considered myself to be above average on the scale when it came to being self-aware and having a relatively objective view of most situations I encountered, including those that were unfolding in my own life. I perceived that I was conscious of my areas of weakness and had been doing the work to improve in the area I felt needed it most at any given time. I pulled no punches and frequently gave myself scathing reviews, after all, I had learned how to approach my failings with stoicism. I was not prepared however for the dissolution of my marriage.

I was a fighter. I faced many difficulties growing up and leading up to my marriage. I had a firm view on what it was supposed to look like, how it should function and I made up my mind early in life that divorce was just not an option for me. I was only ever going to do that one time. I heard stories of Christian couples throughout the years whose marriages had ended in divorce and I was often judgmental. I would sit and assume based on the limited information I had, that one party or the other, maybe even both, weren't truly submitted to God. I figured that that was the root cause of every marital failure. Yet, here I am, seven and a half years later, awaiting the signature of a document that is a court of law's final order officially ending a marriage. To say I felt like a hypocrite and a failure are understatements.

> I was a fighter.

Of course, one does not go through divorce and come out on the other side unscathed. It is a difficult journey I wish on no one. While I do not recommend it, I am also much more understanding of the many factors that are at play and realize that unfortunately, it is likely that more marriages will end this way. Nothing prepares you for the sense of loss and grief you experience despite the difficulties you faced in the union. There is a way in which you become exposed to emotions on a deeper level through the process. It doesn't matter if you are the initiator or not, if you are honest with yourself, you will feel things you've never felt before.

> Letting go has been critical to maintaining my sanity.

Shame, guilt, bitterness, and various levels of depression were just a few of my companions. The failure of my marriage made me feel as though I was disqualified from life. I felt that my purpose was no longer valid and I was destined to live in the shadows. There were some dark days and every now and then, there still are. It seemed like the harder I tried to leave those feelings behind, the closer they clung. Over time I came to realize that I needed to let go if I ever wanted to move on with my life.

Letting go has been critical to maintaining my sanity. Releasing the hurt and pain I felt was inflicted on me and acknowledging that I too had a part to play, helped on the journey of healing. I had to forgive if I wanted to be free. Forgive my husband, forgive others, but most importantly, I had to forgive myself. This was probably the most difficult part of it all. I held myself to an impossibly high standard and was harder on myself than anyone else. How could I have failed? Why couldn't I make it work? Where did I keep going wrong? Maybe I didn't try hard enough. Maybe I should have done something different. I beat up on myself for years and all that did was further the damage that was already present.

> Forgiving yourself brings freedom that you can't receive anywhere else.

Forgiving myself has been a slow but beautiful voyage through what extending grace to myself looks like. Sometimes we read or hear about forgiving others but we rarely stop to think that we are also worthy and deserving of the same treatment we give to those around us. We are often kind and compassionate to those around us, being understanding when they are going through a difficult time. Hardly do we treat ourselves the same way, with kindness, compassion, and love. Forgiving yourself brings freedom that you can't receive anywhere else.

Chapter 8

A New Day Has Dawned

He hath made every thing beautiful in his time:

Ecclesiastes 3:11a

Though the enemy of my soul has laboured tirelessly, whispering lie after well crafted lie to ensure that I would stay in a place that leaves me feeling defeated, here I am, telling my story. I'm writing to let you know, friend, that you are not alone. Our stories may be different but if there is even one parallel, I hope it stirs something within you to take a step toward getting the help you deserve. To give you the nudge to take a step toward getting the help you need. To get out of your head and seek out those around you for guidance on taking the right exit, and going in the right direction. Now is your chance. This is the time to make a

> Don't let guilt or shame keep you bound.

move. Don't let guilt or shame keep you bound. Refuse to allow fear to hold you captive any longer. Forgive yourself and those who have caused you pain.

Having people around that never gave up on me or allowed me to give up on myself was vital to making it through the darkest days.

> Make the decision to do the hard work to heal.

The number of people is nowhere near as important as the sincerity and quality of those in your corner. Each of them prayed for and helped me in practical ways when I couldn't see a way out. This required a measure of vulnerability that was difficult but was truly worth it. Their presence in my life along with that of a professional counselor, helped keep me anchored. Do not be fooled, you can't do it on your own. No matter how self aware or intelligent you are, there are always blind spots, areas in which we are unable to see ourselves clearly. Make the decision to do the hard work to heal.

Each of us has wounds caused from things that have been done or happened to us when we were younger and we need help to identify them and begin the process of healing. Healing is a lifelong journey. For some, that gives the impression of futility but let me assure you that nothing is further from the truth. It is the pursuit of a life of purpose and fulfillment free from the expectations and restrictions of others. One step at a time you walk away from the things that once bound you and toward the peace and joy that awaits.

> No matter how many times you start and stop, know that all it takes is one more step to get started again.

After over a year, here I sit penning this final chapter. I took this book up on so many days thinking, 'I'm going to write today!', but put it back down shortly after thinking, that I had nothing to say. There were so many times that doubt and fear came knocking at my door. 'Who would want to read anything you write? Where is your story of victory?' they would say. Many days I succumbed to their taunts. Today I stand victorious. This journey was never about proving that I had arrived but about being brave enough to finish. This was an exercise in obedience.

I sincerely hope that this will encourage you to take a step of faith. It need not be a leap. One tiny step, an inch at a time, slow but steady. I still have a far way to go. As you have read, I'm clearly not there yet and I doubt that I will ever 'get there' but I have determined in my heart to never stop moving toward that goal. Healing is possible. Help is available. There are people who want to assist, give them room to do so. As I continue on my journey I pray that you will be moved to start yours. No matter how many times you start and stop, know that all it takes is one more step to get started again.

May His grace be sufficient for you, as it has been for me.

www.ingramcontent.com/pod-product-compliance
Lightning Source LLC
LaVergne TN
LVHW051202080426
835508LV00021B/2753